T0326825

STUDY GUIDE FOR

*en*Gendered

STUDY GUIDE FOR

*en*Gendered

God's Gift of
Gender Difference
in Relationship

INCLUDES QUESTIONS FOR GROUP DISCUSSION
AND ANSWER GUIDE FOR LEADERS

SAM A. ANDREADES

LEXHAM PRESS

Study Guide For enGendered: God's Gift of Gender Difference in Relationship
© 2016 by Sam A. Andreades

Lexham Press, 1313 Commercial St., Bellingham, WA 98225
LexhamPress.com

First edition by Weaver Book Company.

Print ISBN 9781683592525
Digital ISBN 9781683592532

Cover: Frank Gutbrod
Interior design and typesetting: Frank Gutbrod

Preface

I am so glad that you are going through *enGendered* with your group. Given the need we have in our time to recognize the gift that gender is to us, prayerful discussion about gender is essential to the church, that we might discern God's wisdom for our lives together. Well-done in making this a topic of exploration for your folks!

This guide includes the following two items: (1) study and discussion questions for each chapter, arranged on one page per chapter so you can reproduce the questions for your group, and (2) an answer guide for you, the leader.

The spacing of the questions on the question pages allows you the option of having the group members write out their answers ahead of the meeting if you would like. They are designed for reading one chapter between each meeting of your group, but you can use them as suits you best. Doing one chapter per week would make for 17–20 weeks, or a 4-to-6 month cycle. By combining chapters you could reduce that, of course.

I pray that God will bless your group's study of biblical gender principles and that your folks will be enabled by your discussions to deeply celebrate the precious gift that He has given us.

Yours in Truth,

Sam Andreades

samandreades@gmail.com

QUESTIONS FOR GROUP DISCUSSION

Introduction:
Prohibitions Are Not Enough

1. What are some puzzling things people say about gender in relationships? What is your question? What do you find confusing or difficult?

2. Do you think that the Bible's negative commands about things affirm something else? What are some examples?

3. Do you think it is possible, as the author asserts, that there are men with same-sex attraction who got married to women and live a long, happily married life? Why do you think this is or is not possible?

4. Have you ever wondered why the Bible says some of the things it says? Which things?

5. From what you understand now, how would you define a real man and a true woman? (Write this answer out).

PART I

CHAPTER I

We Have Lost the Trail
of Relational Love

1. What was that "Big Frolicking Circle stuff before the chapter? Was that whacked out or what? What was the author talking about?

2. The author says that the New Testament makes a big deal about gender in relationship. In fact, he claimed that in the New Testament almost all passages about marriage talk about gender too. Is that true? Can you think of any marriage teachings that do not talk about gender?

3. What passage would you choose (or did you choose) for your wedding?

4. Do you like walking in the woods? Do you think that that is a good analogy for getting into a relationship? Why or why not?

5. Are you aware of the "Gender Studies" efforts of different universities? How do you think that they are helpful or unhelpful?

6. Do you think our church is comfortable talking about gender issues? Why might this be so?

7. Do you think that the Bible can really help us with these things? Why or why not?

The God of Closeness
Has Shown Himself

1. Why do you think it is important to recognize that some relationships are meant to be closer than others, that they run along what might be called a "closeness continuum"?

2. What do you think Genesis 2:24 means when it talks about marriage as two people becoming "one flesh"? How does that relate to what researchers tell us is the key to flourishing marriages?

3. Have you ever thought about the intimacy shared among the members of the Triune Godhead? Which biblical passage, that the author shared or that you think of yourself, helps you to appreciate what is going on inside of God this way?

4. How does it help you to think about your own relationships as mirrors of the relationship within God Themself?

5. Do you believe what Matthew 11:27 and John 14:23 imply, that you could be caught up in the love shared by members of the Trinity? What do you think that is like? What does that tell us about the goal of our earthly relationships?

CHAPTER 3

Gender Is Hard to Talk About for Good Reason

1. If you are a man, would you rather be, if you had to choose, respected or loved? Do you think all men feel as you do? If you are a woman, do you "seek consensus, verbalize and empathize more, and listen better?" Do you think all women are like that?

2. Can you confidently say what makes a man a man or what gives women their womanliness? If you would say "yes," how would you define manhood? Womanliness? Is it anything more than genitalia? If you would say, "no," why do you think that you cannot do something so simple, when men and women are part of our lives every day, all the time?

3. Read Genesis 1:26–27—"So God created man in his own image, in the image of God he created him; male and female he created them." Do the nouns agree in number (singular/plural)? Why is that?

4. What is the difference that the author makes between male/female and masculine/feminine (or man/woman)? Do you think that it is helpful?

They Are Equal in Power and Glory

1. Is it your impression that the Bible preaches that women are equal to men? Where did you get that impression?

2. The author contrasted the Old Testament teaching and then New Testament teaching with the values of the ancient world in which the Scripture documents were written? Why is that helpful to know?

3. Did you find the table on pages 45–46 of *enGendered* to be convincing in showing women's equality in the Bible? Why or why not?

4. What do you think of the statement, "Women have always prophesied in the covenant community" (i.e., among God's people)?

5. Why were men and women created equal?

6. How is their equality important for intimacy?

7. How does our church do in upholding the importance of a woman's perspective?

8. Is there something to be done to improve the way we do things?

CHAPTER 5

Gender Matters in Relationship

1. Revisiting this question from the introduction, can you believe that a man with SSA could be happily married to (including having physical relations) with a woman?

2. What do you think this statement means: "People (meaning men and women) are created in the image of God"? Do you think it is easy to figure out what separates us from animals and angels?

3. Theologians have thought about that previous question a lot. What did the author say that some theologians, especially beginning in the twentieth century, have argued to constitute the image of God in us? Does that make sense to you?

4. According to the author, Jesus says that gender difference causes marriage. Or put another way, "Marriage happens as an expression of gender distinction." Can you explain the author's reasoning for claiming that, using Mark 10, Genesis 2 and Genesis 1? What do you think?

5. Where does the Bible distinguish gender most forcefully? Why is that so?

6. The author tells a story of a single woman who got engaged and how that experience changed her feelings about the New Testament instruction to wives. Do you think that married women can understand that instruction better than single women? Why?

7. Highlighting 1 Corinthians 11:11, the author translates "Woman is not apart from man. Man is not apart from woman" and then says, "Manhood is defined in relation to woman and womanliness in relation to man." What do you think that means?

Sex Differences Form the Platform of God's Gift

1. Are boys different from girls? How? Emotionally? Mentally?

2. What do graphs of sex-related traits (such as the one on page 60) tell us about male-female differences?

3. Why do these features of sex-related traits make it hard to define womanhood or manliness?

4. What three lessons about God's platform of male-female difference do these features of the graph teach us?

5. Does the Bible define gender by male-female differences? Why is the Bible's way more helpful?

6. What can you do differently to walk more closely to the Bible's explanation of gender?

CHAPTER 7

The Grand Asymmetries of Gender Give Us Specialties

1. Where is the best source of teaching on the meaning of the creation of gender in Genesis 2?

2. What is the key word the author uses to describe the differences between men and women? What are the three the apostle Paul points out? Where does he cite them?

3. Does the meaning of "firstborn" explained by the author make sense to you? How do you see that making a difference between Adam and Eve's treatment of each other?

4. Adam found his home in Eve and Eve found her security in Adam. Have you experienced one of these? How so?

5. Does it make sense to you that God made man and woman for different purposes in His mission on the earth? How would you describe, based on what Genesis 2 says, those different purposes?

6. Which of the three asymmetries do you find happening in your marriage or close relationships with the other gender? Which of them do you struggle with? If you do, why do you think that is so?

The Asymmetry of Origin: The Man of the Solid Ground and the Woman of the Resting Rib

1. The author gives a number of scriptural illustrations for masculine securing and feminine giving rest. Which of these (or others that you see) is most convincing or moving to you?

2. What do the beginning and ending of *Judges* show us? Does it make sense to you to gauge a society by how its women are treated?

3. Is it helpful to think about how there are different ways to fulfill the gender call to secure and give rest? How so?

4. What are some ways you have acted as a man to make the close woman or women in your life secure? What are ways you can do this better?

5. What are some ways you have acted as a woman to give rest to the close man or men in your life? What are ways you can do this better?

6. As a man, are you ready to frankly ask the close woman in your life what makes her secure? As a woman, are you ready to ask your man what gives him rest? What if you don't feel like doing these things?

CHAPTER 9

The Asymmetry of Order (Part 1): The Firstborn

1. What do the parallel episodes of the daughters of Zelophehad (Num. 27:1–11) and the sons of Gilead (Num. 36:1–12) teach us about gender in the ancient covenant community of Israel? What did the laws cause in the community?

2. Is it helpful to you to see the dual principles of equality and asymmetry throughout the Scriptures? Do you think that it strikes an important balance?

3. Describe being in charge in Jesus' Kingdom. Do you want to be?

4. Are you convinced by the author's exegesis of Peter's "the wife as weaker vessel" passage? Why would it be helpful or valuable to think of it this way?

5. What are ways you, as a husband or brother, can enact your firstborn authority?

6. Specifically, as a husband, how can you fulfill Ephesians 5:26 (washing by word)?

7. Part of the role of the Firstborn, or Head, is representation. How did Jesus represent His bride (the church)? How can you, as a husband?

8. What do you get from being a man to the women in your life?

The Asymmetry of Order (Part 2): The Promoter

1. According to the author, what are three important features of submission?

2. What is the synonym for submission that highlights its nature as a gift in relationship? Why is this a helpful way of looking at it?

3. Does it take strength to submit to someone? Have you seen this need for strength in your life?

4. Does one have to be very engaged to biblically submit or is it a passive activity? Explain why this is so.

5. If appropriate to share, in what ways do you as a woman believe you should submit that you currently are not?

6. As a woman, how does it help to visualize Christ standing behind your husband, asking you to submit?

7. What are some ways you, as a wife or sister, can enact your call to promote a close man?

CHAPTER 11

The Asymmetry of Intent: The Commissioned and the Empowerer

1. Why did you get married (or why do you want to get married if you do)?

2. Why did God get you married (or why will God get you married if He does)?

3. Where are some ways, do you think, that feminism has missed the boat of God's purposes? How can these hurt women?

4. In the following examples, how did the woman help the man to rise? Achsah helping Othniel? Deborah helping Barak? Abigail helping David? The Proverbs 31 wife helping her husband? Priscilla helping Apollos?

5. Can you say what the mission of your marriage and family is? Can you commit to talking and praying about it?

6. What is one way you can, as a woman, empower the mission of your marriage, or, as a man, apprehend and lead in the mission of your marriage?

7. From what you understand now, how would you define a real man and a true woman? (Write out your answer to this question.)

Gender Specialties:
Banishing Independence

1. What do you think of these "scenic overlooks" that begin many of these chapters? Do they help you envision how gender works?

2. What are some examples of things we all are called to do that are also things that some people specialize in?

3. Does thinking of gender working through specialties help you to see how to be gendered? If so, how?

4. When should "gender trump gifting"? Can you think of a time when that happened in your life?

5. What did you think of the questions of "Dan" and "Danielle" in the text? Do you agree with the author's answer about needing the other gender to know our own?

6. How did your definitions of a real man and a true woman from last time compare with the author's? Do you think the text's definitions are helpful? Why or why not?

CHAPTER 13
Culture: The Clothes of Gender

1. Did you notice anything a bit off about the picture on the book's cover? What do you think that is saying?

2. Do you like football? What does it have to do with being a man?

3. In a candied apple, which is culture and which is gender? What happens when we mistake the cultural practice for the underlying reality of gender itself?

4. The author gives an extended discussion of 1Corinthians 11:2–16 because it "explains the relationship of gender and culture." What did you get out of that?

5. How should we defy our own culture (like Paul did in having women speak in church)? What cultural practices should we reject because they speak falsely about gender?

6. How would we wear our culture into worship (like Paul did w/head coverings)? What cultural practices should we embrace because they speak truly about gender?

The Purpose of the Genders: A Gift to Foster Intimacy

1. Did you realize that marriage as an institution is in trouble? Why do you think that this is so?

2. The author identifies strongly identifying Christians (i.e., who actually follow Christ, go to church, etc.), as having lower divorce rates and higher marital happiness. Why do you think that is? What does the author identify as the thing such Christian couples do that is different?

3. What are some of the outcomes in the Bible from gendered behavior?

4. What does the different "therefore" of Jesus' and Paul's quoting Genesis 2:24 teach us about the purpose of gender in marriage?

In preparation for next week:

5. How would you define emotional intimacy?

Deeper Still: Dynamics of Intergendered Intimacy

1. Is it easy or hard to define emotional intimacy? Why do you think that this is so?

2. How did your definition of intimacy compare to the author's? What are "the seven facets of the jewel" of intimacy? Do you think that they get it? Would you add or subtract any?

3. Which facet of intimacy means the most to you? Why is it good to be aware of all of them in speaking about intimacy?

4. How does gender difference cultivate these different facets of intimacy? Does it make sense to you that God would ordain our close romantic relationships to be intergendered?

5. How did the challenge of loving one of a different gender (a wife) make the men in the book grow into who they were?

6. How has the challenge of loving one of a different gender helped you to grow?

CHAPTER 16

Sex: Respecting the Platform
of Distinction

1. What do the different stories of those with SSA teach us about our sexuality?

2. Could something that was bad and wrong for us still be beneficial to us? How could this be?

3. Is anyone born gay?

4. Is it possible for someone with SSA to ever have a happy sexual relationship with a woman?

5. What do Sodom and Gomorrah show us about God's image and forbidden sexual desires? What did God desire for the people of those cities?

6. The author asserts "gender asymmetries arouse." What does that mean?

7. Do you like eating chocolate with peanut butter?

Continuum of Closeness: When Gender Does and Doesn't Matter

1. Do you see the Old Testament and New Testament distinguishing gender outside of marriage?

2. Can you think of examples you have seen of genderly acts by spiritual or physical brothers and sisters?

3. Where does gender not matter? Can you give some examples?

4. What are the three ways the author gives for single people to experience intimacy?

5. If you are single, are these ways attractive to you? Do you value your singleness?

CHAPTER 18

The Immense Invitation

1. When the New Testament talks about marriage, which role, husband or wife, is compared to Jesus Christ?

2. In what ways do you think Christ, as the Second member of the Trinity, acts genderly toward the First?

3. Are people living more independently and less intimately? What do you think of the author's statement, "the more independent we become, women or men, the more intimacy eludes us"?

4. According to Ephesians 5, what are the missions to which a husband and wife should more and more aspire?

5. What does God ultimately want for us?

ANSWER GUIDE FOR LEADERS

Introduction:
Prohibitions Are Not Enough

1. *Puzzling things.* The point of this question is to draw out the concerns and positions of people in the group. The book's back cover and chapter headings give some of these problems that are widespread. Expect to hear things like:

   "Why would God keep my gay friend from true love in a monogamous life-long relationship?"

   "Why would the Bible tell me to deny my same-sex desires when I did not ask for them?"

   "Why do I feel embarrassed saying women/girls are different from men/boys?"

   "Why should I/my mom submit to him/my dad in decision-making when I am/she is a better decision-maker?"

   "Does the Bible really tell women to wear head coverings to church?"

   "Does a man have the same relationship with Jesus that I as a woman have?"

   "If I am a lesbian, does Jesus accept me 'Just as I Am'?"

   "Can't I find a woman who is not so high-maintenance?"

   "How come I cannot get my husband to stand up to people for us?"

   "Why don't I sing about being a man?"

   "Doesn't the Bible denigrate women?"

   "How come I can't find a good passage for our wedding?"

   "In the end, you need to look out for yourself. No one else can do it for you, right?"

   "What do you want me to do, stay home and bake cookies?"

   "Jesus never talks about homosexuality, does He?"

   "Does the apostle Paul have a thing against empowering women?"

   "What's wrong with cross-dressing?"

   "What will make my marriage last?"

   "Why can't she just trust me?"

   "How come the guys in church don't listen to me?"

   "I desire love more than respect. Is there something wrong with me as a man?"

   "I thought boys were good at math but then why is my wife is a nuclear physicist?"

   "It isn't possible for a homosexual man to enjoy sex with a woman . . . is it?"

   "Why can't she get off my back about reading to the kids-I don't feel like it."

   "Should we have a knitting group ministry for gals in our church?"

   "Shouldn't I be excused as a man for using porn because men are naturally more sexual?"

   "Why can't Doug just grow up?"

   "Should I be worried that Peggy spends all her spare time on football?"

"Is it fair for a man with same-sex attraction to marry a woman?"
"Does God want me as a man to open the door for my women acquaintances?"
"Where is my job description as a husband in this marriage thing?"
"As a single, am I not a full person?"
"Can't you see that I was born this way?"
"How do I invigorate sex life with my spouse?"
"I am getting married to be happy. Is that so bad?"
"How could depending on her make me more me?"
"What does God have to do with my love life?"

Note where your folks are and to what questions they need answers.

2. *Negatives affirming something else.* This truth about God's prohibitions is an important point to get in order to help people build a theology of gender.

Good examples:
"Thou shalt not bear false witness!" → Exalting Truthfulness in God's character.
"Don't have sex outside of marriage—what the Bible calls 'fornication' or 'sexual immorality.'" → This is actually exalting sex, not demeaning it. Sex is such a beautiful, exalted, weighty gift, God wants us to hold it as sacred and enjoy it properly.
"Thou shalt not take the name of the Lord Thy God in vain." → God is so holy, we should desire to treat Him with reverence and awe.

Encourage thinking about other examples.

3. *Same-sex attracted men married to women.* Increasingly, because of the gay narrative, young people believe that "orientation" is inborn, inherent and immutable. That idea should be challenged (as it is in the book by scientific, sociological and biblical references) to give hope and challenge to those who find their desires contrary to the Bible's teaching.

4. *Puzzling things in Bible.* This is an open-ended question to determine if there are problem passages about gender in the Bible among your folks (and yes, you can assume that there are).

5. *Defining a real man and a true woman.* Get them to write down their name and what they think now and collect the answers. You don't need to discuss now. We'll be looking later on at how these answers might change over the course of the study.

We Have Lost the Trail
of Relational Love

1. *"Frolicking Circle."* It is fun to hear peoples' reactions to that opening scene. As explained later in the book, the description visualizes Proverbs 8. "Circle on the face of the deep" comes from Proverbs 8:27. The scene is a scientific and poetic imagining of what went on between the Second (the Wisdom of God) and the First (the Master Creator) when they began the universe, and all was being prepared for the crowning creation of humanity. Did some folks grasp that?

2. *New Testament marriage passages are about gender.* See if anyone can come up with Hebrews 13:4 (about the marriage bed). Otherwise it is all about gender, even the divorce passages really, because they show the New Testament value of equality among women and men. The prominence of gender should hopefully get folks thinking about how important gender is to close relationships, according to the Scriptures.

3. *Their wedding passage:* Get young adults thinking about it early! Listen to why married couples (or their ministers) chose what they did to honor their union.

4. *Walking in the woods-relationship analogy.* Evaluating the woods analogy can make for open-ended discussion, simply to hear peoples' thoughts on relationships.

5. *Gender Studies.* If appropriate, inquiring about "Gender Studies" can educate you on what your people are hearing "out there." Perhaps someone has studied these things herself or has been influenced by gender studies. It is good to engage with the culture. Researchers' explore the difficulties of gender, even if they only get part of the truth or get it wrong.

6. *Church talking about gender issues.* This question should be asked in every church. It can lead to a discussion of the effect of our culture on the church. Are people afraid to talk about gender? Do they feel like they don't know how to? Is there concern about causing division? Do leaders not ask because they don't want to hear the answers? How are we doing in not capitulating to, nor running from, our culture?

7. *The Bible helping us with gender.* It is good to take the temperature of our folks on their attitudes toward Scripture's authority and sufficiency. Do they lack confidence in it? Do they question the Bible's relevance?

CHAPTER 2

The God of Closeness Has Shown Himself

1. *Closeness continuum.* The notion of a "closeness continuum" becomes important later in the book, as we learn about how gender matters in relationship, so the closer the relationship, the more gender matters. It is also key to appreciate when gender doesn't matter. So it is good to get clear in our minds early. For now, you can expect answers like "I don't see the big deal," or "It is important so we don't spend a lot of time developing relationships that should remain just as acquaintances." Some point out that social media can encourage sharing with others what might not be appropriate.

2. *Genesis 2:24 and the one flesh profundity.* The answer is intimacy, though people may talk about it in different ways (ch. 15 describes the many terms or facets of intimacy). People may be used to thinking "one flesh" just means sex, so the discussion may help them broaden their interpretation to include emotional intimacy as well. Seeing that both the Bible and sociologists recognize emotional intimacy as key to flourishing marriages helps to prepare us to appreciate what is going on inside of God and what He wants for us.

3. *The Trinity's intimacy.* Chapter 2 tours several passages that draw back the curtain on some of what goes on between members of the Trinity of God. (The first page of the Appendix—page 192—gives such a list.)

4. Hopefully one or more of them has helped the readers to think more deeply about how our human relationships are just mirrors of what goes on in God.

5. *Relationships as mirrors of God Themself.* Hopefully, this way of thinking, that their human relationships mirror what is going on in God, will help folks to understand God better (Praise the Lord!), and also to esteem the relationships He has given them. It can also guide them to godliness in their relationships. Encourage all three directions of thought.

6. *Being caught up in the Trinity's intimacy.* This question encourages theological dreaming about Christ's promise to reveal the First member of God in a way that approaches how Christ knows Him (Matt. 11:27), and to have the two of Them make their home in us (John 14:23). We might normally read those passages to mean simply knowing God in salvation, but our salvation is a progression of knowing God better and better.

CHAPTER 3

Gender Is Hard to Talk About for Good Reason

NB: The four suggested questions below are fairly in-depth, so you may want to take them slowly. Chapter 3 does some important foundational work which is then used throughout the book. So it is good ruminate on the principles for a while.

1. *Respected or loved.* This question can get the juices going about how not all men fit our personal definitions of manhood, and the same for womanliness. That should get people questioning whether they know what gender is.

2. *What makes a man/woman.* Give as much time as necessary to this key question. It is designed to help people come to the realization that it is impossible (apart from the Bible) to define our genders. The way to do this is to let someone proffer a definition and then let others question it until it dies a death by a million qualifications. Most of us carry around an "essentialist" idea of manhood or womanliness, that is, that it consists of some essential qualities that all men or all women share. To appreciate the Bible's wisdom, it is necessary to show how such definitions are inadequate to encompass what God has created.

3. *Genesis 1 singular/plurals.* No they don't agree. Foster a discussion to get people to think about how awkward gender is even when God explains it Himself in His word. The answer is: you do not have the fullness of one gender without the other. This is explicitly stated in 1Corinthians 11:11.

4. *Male/Female-Masculine/Feminine distinction.* Answer: Male/Female = physical, biological differences, our dust nature that we share with the animals, the platform of gender (to which we return in ch. 6). Masculine/Feminine = gender, the image of God in us, bestowed on us by the breath of God. Physical, sexual difference existed before, in plants and animals, but gender is new. It is uniquely human.

This distinction is helpful for several reasons: First it helps us appreciate the majesty of the subject under discussion. We are given a unique gift of God in being human! It also helps us avoid different errors that will unfold in the book:

   a. Besides different genitalia, male-female sexual differences overlap. (These are sometimes called secondary sex traits.) Sometimes what is typical for a female, like being nurturing or being shorter, shows up in a male instead. God loves this kind of variety. But if we think that the typical sexual trait is what makes a woman, we can mess people up. We might exclude people by our expectations, or look down on them. Gender is not a set of essential traits but a call to godliness in a certain style with the traits we are given.

   b. Another error of confusing sexual differences with gender is seeing sexual differences as our guide to behavior in relationship. E.g., "Guys should be excused from using porn because they are more sexual."

   c. If your gender is just your genitalia, medical procedures have gotten quite good. So if you have the money and inclination, you start to believe that you can just change it.

People may not think of these, or may think of others, which is fine.

CHAPTER 4

They Are Equal in Power and Glory

1. *Impressions about the Bible on equality.* This question should help you determine peoples' view of the Bible on women. Have they gotten these views from their own reading or from what other people say about the Bible? If certain passages cause problems for them, you can ask them to be patient as we may deal with these passages later. Such passages may be teaching about gender asymmetry while not impinging on biblical equality.

2. *Scripture's contrast with its surrounding cultures.* Hopefully, the book has conveyed just how radical the Bible has been down through the ages on insisting on women's equality and importance to God. If women feel demeaned, this point about the Bible is a powerfully healing balm. It also helps establish the Scriptures as a consistent counter-cultural force of truth in all that it says about gender.

3. *The table showing points on equality in Scripture.* Again, the Bible's insistence on women's equality is critical for understanding its teaching about asymmetry (to come in Part 2) and to prevent situations of abuse that occur all too often. So you should lead the group in driving this point home.

4. *"Women have always prophesied . . ."* If needed review the scriptural examples given in the book. Whatever one's view of prophecy, this feature of the Bible makes a powerful point about how God wants women involved in His goings-on. Though no women are ever made priests or kings, showing an asymmetry (discussed in Part 2), God uses women specifically in speaking needed truth.

5. *Why men and women were created equal.* This question is designed to take us back to the Trinity of God, and a crucial truth about Members of the Godhead. Women and men are created equal because the First, Second, and Third Members are equal. This has many implications both for how we understand Christ and Holy Spirit as well as how we conduct our relationships. Guide folks to explore some of these in your conversation. Sometimes people wonder, is God a man or a woman? The answer, according to 1 Corintians 11:12, is that God contains both the masculine and the feminine.

6. *How equality is important for intimacy.* Deep intimacy can only really be achieved among equals. God wants us to know that intimacy in our inter-gendered relationships. Perhaps your group can think together about why that is, comparing unequal relationships to equal ones.

7. *How your church is doing.* Be prepared for people to express strong feelings on this question. Women may feel stifled and misunderstood in your church. Others may be worried that even talking about women's equality might take us overboard in making no distinctions at all in what men and women do in church. Simply listening might be a good first step.

8. *Application question.* If appropriate, perhaps your people can hypothesize better practices that can be listed and evaluated as you go through the book's points together.

CHAPTER 5

Gender Matters in Relationship

1. *Marriages with one partner with SSA.* If people cannot imagine such a marriage (what research literature calls "mixed orientation marriages"), they have fallen prey to the cultural falsehood that gayness is an inherent and inviolable trait of a person. Try to help them see that we are all sexually deviant in one way or another—desiring to have sex with someone who is not your spouse is just as bad a departure from God's way (Matt. 5:28) as desiring to have sex with someone of the same gender. Yet we do not (and should not) accept that deviance of sexual desire as part of our identity.

2. *The meaning of the "image of God."* The book's endnote 1 on page 210 cites the three basic ways theologians have defined *imago Dei*: as having attributes like God, taking dominion like God, and being in relationship like God. This could be a long discussion: when you start to think about it, it is difficult to pin down the meaning.

3. *The twentieth century emphasis on the image of God as being in relationship.* It is good to focus on this premise because we build upon this foundational understanding that we have relationships because God has relationship within Themself.

4. *Jesus saying that gender difference causes marriage.* This is a key exegetical point so it pays to make sure people know where it is coming from, following the book closely. Help folks to see how the Markan passage uses the two Genesis texts. If your group contains single folks, it may be important to re-assert, as book does, that gender does matter in single people also, even if they do not get married, because they have other close relationships.

5. *Where the Bible distinguishes gender most forcefully.* The Bible distinguishes gender most forcefully in the context of marriage because marriage is such an intense relationship. This is good time to introduce the idea that gender is a gift, a specialty, for developing another person in relationship: an important key to the universe.

6. *Being married helping one better appreciate New Testament teaching such as submission.* It is revealing to hear about peoples' attitudes toward New Testament teachings as they grow and especially what happens as they get married. The teachings often start to make much more sense when one gets close to a spouse or sibling, where gender matters.

7. *"Woman is not apart from man. . ." (1 Cor. 11:11).* This profound statement is worth contemplating. We hope that people can understand it in a deeper way than just that the first woman was made from Adam and that men are now born from women. Rather, one needs the other for its definition.

CHAPTER 6
Sex Differences Form the Platform of God's Gift

1. *How boys are different from girls.* This is a fun discussion because we all notice some different things and have our own essentialist theories, and all of them have annoying exceptions among people we may meet. The discussion should help prepare people for the understanding that gender, masculinity/femininity, is something more than male/female traits.

2. *The overlapping graphs of sex-related traits.* They tell us that sex differences can be quite small. And they tell us that the statistical distributions in men and women always overlap. So it is always incorrect to say, "All men are Y" and "All women are X" unless you are speaking about chromosomes. Even chromosomally, there are in rare occurrences birth defects. These exceptions are tragedies that need compassionate care to correct.

3. *Why this makes it hard to define womanhood/manliness.* As soon as you define gender by these traits you exclude some.

4. *Three lessons about God's platform of male-female difference.* The answer is on page 64: It makes connecting possible. It displays God's love of variety. It calls us to include the exceptional.

5. *How the Bible does not define gender by male-female differences.* The Bible's way is more helpful because it teaches not to use biology as a guide and it doesn't exclude people. Instead the Bible's direction encourages people to be whom God made them to be.

6. *Applying the Bible's explanation of gender.* Be sure to give time to (and help) people to plan how to act differently based on these convictions. Perhaps you can take note and keep them accountable by asking how it went the next few times you meet.

PART 2

CHAPTER 7

The Grand Asymmetries of Gender Give Us Specialties

1. *The best source of teaching on Genesis 2.* The Bible itself, of course! Specifically, the apostle Paul, whom God chose to shape our Christian understanding in the New Testament. Considering this point can help us cut through the clutter of opinions that fuel much of the debate about gender distinction in the church.

2. *The key word describing differences and the three found in Paul.* "Asymmetry" is the descriptive word I use. First Timothy 2:12-13 and 1 Corinthians 11:7–10 are the explicit places where Paul cites the three asymmetries in the creation of the man and the woman:
   a. The order of being created: The Firstborn and the Promoter
   b. The way of being created: The Man of the Solid Earth and the Woman of the Resting Rib
   c. The purpose of being created: The Commissioned and the Empowerer

3. *The meaning of "firstborn" and the difference that makes between Adam and Eve.* This question is to help your folks explore the first part of headship, before it is covered in the chapters following. The cultural context of the first-born of a family should be helpful to understand the authority God assigns to the man in relationship.

4. *Experiences to help identify with Adam's experience of finding home and Eve's being secured.* Hopefully folks have had some experience in family or marriage to help them understand Genesis 2. Encourage them to trace their relationships back to the original creation through this question.

5. *Different purposes for the genders in mission.* Even though the text of Genesis 2 is explicit in stating the different purposes for making the man and the woman, this insight does not seem to be well-appreciated in our day. Try to get people thinking, especially the men, about ways they should be stepping up to determine what the family's mission is. Hopefully both men and women in your group can better grasp that they were brought together for a purpose.

6. *Experience of, and struggle with, the three asymmetries.* Get ready for some lively discussion on this question. You are turning a rock over that does not often see the light of day in churches. Listen to the frustrations, puzzlements, fears and, hopefully also, celebrations, and take note for how you can pray for your folks. You can conclude with a call for patience, as difficulties that folks may be bringing up will probably be addressed in the remaining chapters of Part 2.

The Asymmetry of Origin: The Man of the Solid Ground and the Woman of the Resting Rib

1. *Scriptural illustrations for masculine securing and feminine giving rest.* Some people are more comfortable thinking, others more motivated in feeling. The phrasing "convincing" *or* "moving" allows each type to respond to the Scriptures presented in their way. The Bible both makes sense and is emotionally compelling, so both motivations help us to dwell on its pictures of men and women acting genderly toward one another.

2. *The beginning and ending of Judges and how to gauge a society.* The answer, as the book argues, is that at the start, in the era of Joshua, women are prized, but at the end, in the era of Samson, women are treated horribly. You might read Judges 19-21 together with an eye toward how women are being treated. The author's purpose is to show the deterioration of Israelite society under the non-committing judges. Since the care of women is how the author portrays God's judgment of things, we should adopt the biblical worldview of judging our own society by similar measure. How do folks think our culture is doing?

3. *How there are different ways to fulfill the gender call to secure and give rest.* This question can get people thinking about how, in the variety of God's creation, husbands and wives might do things differently. The point, again from chapter five, is that gender matters in relationship, and so how you secure or give rest depends very much on the other person with whom you are in relationship.

4. *and 5. Ways you have done this and ways you should do this.* These two queries are really four questions, two for the men and two for the women, two about the past, two about the future. They allow you to both encourage, and introduce accountability with, your people. With all these gender asymmetries, you should encourage folks in ways they have already been doing them. You should also help them think practically about how to grow in love by intentionally doing better. Again, is there a way for you to introduce accountability for these things in the group?

6. *Asking our spouses or siblings what would help them.* Anything we can do to help communication across lines of gender should be encouraged. Relationships, like walking in the woods, is a journey of exploration and discovery. Let's go! Also, though, be ready for those who don't want to ask because they don't want to do what they might hear as the answer. Those folks may need a challenge to love by the power of Christ.

CHAPTER 9

The Asymmetry of Order (Part 1): The Firstborn

1. *The parallel episodes of the daughters of Zelophehad.* The episodes of *Numbers* teach us equality and asymmetry, the two principles of gender all Christians should use to help them interpret their Bible as they read it. The laws caused men and women to need each other in preserving the tribal lands.

2. *The dual principles of equality and asymmetry throughout the Scriptures.* Hopefully, seeing these two principles played out again and again among God's people can create a framework for thinking and acting genderly with one another.

3. *Being in charge in Jesus' Kingdom.* This question should direct men (and women also) to see that being in charge is not all it is cracked up to be. What God expects of heads, leaders, is laying down their life for their charge, which is not so fun when you get into it.

4. *Peter's "the wife as weaker vessel" passage.* People may have a hard time reading the passage the way I advocate, because we tend to gravitate towards essentialist thinking about gender: men have these qualities, and women have these. And because men usually *are* physically stronger than women (remember sexual difference distributions of chapter six). And because they have read the passage a certain way for a long time. So it is easy to read Peter as saying that wives are essentially weaker. But hopefully considering the particular and peculiar imagery he uses, along with the way the book's recommended reading fits with the rest of the Bible's teaching, will help persuade them that weaker means being in the submissive position.

   Interpreting the passage this way is helpful because it calls men to really appreciate women's vulnerability in submitting so they treat them more carefully.

5. *Ways to enact firstborn authority.* Application time. It does us no good as Christians to learn something new if we do not put it into practice. And we can because we have the Holy Spirit. Just give them time to come up with ways.

6. *Fulfilling Ephesians 5:26 (washing by word) as a husband.* I highlight this way in the book because, one, our quintessential marriage passage does, and two, it is the place of challenge for many husbands. We need to be interrupt-able and pay attention to our wives' need to be washed at inopportune times. What Scripture can help her see clearly in her current crisis? What words can apply balm to her woes?

7. *Representation as head and how Jesus did it.* Hopefully, Jesus taking that ultimate representation for our own sin (2 Cor. 5:21) can inspire us to take steps of representative responsibility for our households.

8. *What we get from being a man.* God is so very gracious that He never requires anything without abundant reward following. And the returns for acting as men are huge. Especially in terms of the effect on the women in our lives. Help men to see that to encourage them in the way of gender.

CHAPTER 10

The Asymmetry of Order (Part 2): The Promoter

1. *The three important features of submission.* A gift, a feat of strength, and an active engagement. Getting these straight helps us frame the discussion in terms of relationship, rather than a task for us to take on in isolation. We always act genderly *for* someone in particular.
2. *The synonym for submission.* "Promotion" is the word that highlights this call's nature as a gift in relationship. Many women find it helpful because the word gives them some good to strive for, a vision for what they accomplish by this hard task. They are doing it *for* someone close to them.
3. *Strength to submit to someone.* Submitting/Promoting certainly is a feat of strength. All people, women or men, should have had some experience in the need to submit, and understand how difficult it is. This discussion should help both men and women, the former to appreciate what their wives or sisters are being asked to do, and the latter to see the value of God's way for us.
4. *Submission/promotion as active and not passive.* This question is to contradict the characterization of the submissive wife as a doormat. To do it right, a woman must actively discern what God considers right, so she can submit "as to the Lord." This is not always easy or clear, but it is the skill needed and the ability in which to grow.
5. *Ways to submit.* Again, it is application time. How can we do this where we are not doing it?
6. *Visualizing Christ standing behind the husband.* This suggestion is one way to bring Jesus into the struggle when you really do not want to promote your husband to first-born authority (or, by the same token, your boss at work—Colossians 3:22). Explore with your folks if this visualization exercise can help in those situations.
7. *Ways to enact the call to promote.* Another application discussion. Hopefully the discussion can help the women to think of ways to actively grow in her gender.

The Asymmetry of Intent: The Commissioned and the Empowerer

1. and 2. *Why you got, or want to get, married, and what God thinks.* These two questions should help folks realize that they might be thinking different things than God about their marriage, and to help them begin to think of their present or future marriage as having a purpose, a mission. God has a Kingdom purpose for them being together, usually including children (e.g., Mal. 2:15).

3. *Feminism's errors and how they hurt us.* A prime mistake of feminism, as it has come to develop, is its tenet that equality for women in society will be achieved if the distinctions between men and women are erased. Another is to encourage women to pursue the worldly meaning of success, the very idol that has enchained so many men. Climbing a career ladder to nowhere, rather than identifying and pursuing God's mission for us, hurts us all.

4. *The biblical examples (Achsah and Othniel, Deborah and Barak, Abigail and David, the Proverbs 31 wife and her husband, Priscilla and Apollos) of women serving the mission that men close to them have identified.* Hopefully, discussing these illustrations from Scripture can give women a vision for this gender distinction, and inspire men in their responsibility here also, to find out what the God's mission is for them and to lead in it.

5. *The mission of your marriage and family.* Expect a lot of ums and aws and silence as folks are put on the spot. After a time of discomfort, tell your folks that this is not an easy or quick question to answer and ask them to commit to praying about and discussing it. Is there a way to hold them accountable for doing that, such as telling them you will ask again in two weeks or a month?

6. *A woman, empowering, or a man, leading, in your marriage's mission.* When people do have a sense of what they believe that God wants for them, it is helpful to help them think about how to take steps in it, what decisions it effects, what it might mean for their schedules, etc.

7. *Defining a real man and a true woman.* Recall this same question from Week #1. It should be fun to hear their answers now. Get out their answers from the Introduction Meeting when you asked this question at first and maybe pass them out. Have any changed? (Hopefully, yes!) Also note, if they have not read ahead yet, if any are able to anticipate the definitions coming in chapter 12. This is really preparation for reading the next chapter, when they will be reading the author's definitions, to discuss next time.

Gender Specialties:
Banishing Independence

1. *"Scenic overlooks" that begin some chapters.* Hopefully, these little vignettes are creating a vision of the beauty of gender as God made it. They involve a lot of historical background research to help us step into the Bible's stories. And they are also supposed to be fun as Christian readers can try to figure out who the characters are before they are revealed in the end.

2. *Examples of things we all are called to do that are also things that some people specialize in.* Many examples could be cited, e.g., preaching the gospel, serving the disadvantaged, handling finances, etc., besides what is cited in the text: the submitting of Ephesians 5:21 and 22. This primes the pump for the next question.

3. *Thinking of gender working through specialties.* A discussion to get folks comfortable with gender distinction as a calling to love one another rather a set of rigid rules.

4. *When "gender should trump gifting."* The answer folks should come to is that it should be done when it will advance the relationship. Hopefully, examples from their lives can illuminate when elevating gender specialties accomplished something special for them. Are there any you can share with them?

5. *The questions of "Dan" and "Danielle" in the text.* The key concept is interdependence. God gave us gender to grow interdependent with one another. It is very unhelpful to talk about gender in isolation. This leads to the definitions following.

6. *Definitions of a real man and a true woman.* Are folks tracking with this way of looking at gender? If not, why? What might be the real (unspoken) issue?

Culture: The Clothes of Gender

1. *The picture on the book's cover.* The man's shoes are reversed (left and right) and the woman's are two left shoes. Because our gender is so awkward to wear these days. Things feel reversed.
2. *Football and what it has to do with being a man.* This is to get folks thinking about the difference between gender and the cultural practices it is dressed in.
3. *The candied apple analogy.* If we don't distinguish, we can exclude people because they don't fit the cultural stereotype. We can also adopt non-biblical principles and expectations, adding to the word of God, and getting stuff caught in our teeth.
4. *Discussion of 1 Corinthians 11:2–16 and the relationship of gender and culture.* This can be a confusing topic, but hopefully we can read the apostle's wisdom here to see that, based on gender principles we know, equality and asymmetry, we should reject some cultural customs and embrace others. Paul rejected the practice of excluding women from the church service and embraced the practice of head coverings. We should do likewise with our own culture.
5. *Defying our culture.* It is good to hear what folks are aware of going on now that contradicts the principles of gender. Learn from them on this one.
6. *Embracing our culture when it speaks truly about gender.* This side of things, the head covering side, is just as important to emphasize. We should approve of what is excellent (Phil. 1:10).

CHAPTER 14

The Purpose of the Genders: A Gift to Foster Intimacy

1. *How marriage is in trouble.* See if people recognize the recession of intimacy in relationships.
2. *Divorce rates, marital happiness, and the edge Christian couples seem to have.* Christian couples that practice gender distinction have better marriages. This fact should prepare the way for the final tenet of gender in the book: that gender distinction is a gift from God to foster intimacy among us. Along with the Bible (next question), the marriage statistics and studies support the principle.
3. *Outcomes in the Bible from gendered behavior.* A Review question. What we want them to remember is that gender is very powerful. It can convert people (1 Peter 3:1) and sanctify people (Eph. 5:25–27). It may help to go and look at some of the passages cited on page 153.
4. *The different use of "therefore" by Jesus and Paul (one cause and one purpose) in quoting Genesis 2:24.* Jesus said that gender causes marriage. Paul says that marriage's purpose is intimacy. This leads now to the last tenet of our theology of gender: Gender difference makes for intimacy. This is a point to ponder and for which to give God praise.
5. *Their defining emotional intimacy.* Having them do this before they read the next chapter can enhance the realization that defining all that intimacy entails is no easy thing.

Deeper Still: Dynamics of Intergendered Intimacy

1. *The difficulty of defining intimacy.* Again, the difficulty is in how we are discovering something about God. To have relationships is to be made in God's image, so emotional intimacy reflects what is happening in God Themself.

2. *"The seven facets of the jewel" of intimacy.* It is good to hear if your folks think that these seven capture what emotional intimacy is about, because the chapter then builds a social science argument for how gender distinction in marriage cultivates these. If they feel that something is missing, or one of them is unnecessary to the experience of intimacy, it would be good to know. I'd be surprised if someone identified another facet, but could be.

3. *Which facet of intimacy means the most to you.* I predict that you will, as I did in the DSM study, get different answers to this question. Because different ones are more or less important to different people. Some really value sharing, others trust, others companionship. Probably this has to do with different personalities and different histories.

4. *How gender difference cultivates different facets of intimacy.* The chapter lists many different ways (28, to be exact). Hopefully folks can recall a few of them that stood out as they read. Does it make sense to them that God created marriage this way? It is the beauty of this experience that is the positive good He wants for us in forbidding same-sex marriage.

5. *The challenge of loving one of a different gender (a wife) making the men in the book grow into who they were.* The book quotes a number of the guys' words about how they grew into more of who they were through the challenge of the other. It is good to bring this dynamic out to realize the enormous value of the gift of intergendered relationships for us.

6. *How the challenge has helped them to grow.* Hopefully, some or all of the group has experienced something like this in their own life in different ways. If they are married, they should be able to cite how trying to love their spouse has stretched them.

CHAPTER 16

Sex: Respecting the Platform
of Distinction

1. *The different stories of those with SSA and what they teach us about our sexuality.* The answer here is that our sexuality is complex. It is not something we are born with, but develops through our early life, shaped by many different factors. God has given us a rich and beautiful expression of our identities in our sexuality. And, unfortunately, all that is wrong with our identities is also expressed in sex.
2. *Something being bad and wrong for us yet still beneficial to us.* This is a question to bring out the resilience and power of the goodness of God's creation. His work is so good, it is hard to kill it. Even as we twist and misuse His gifts through sin, they still offer benefits to us. Because of the goodness of God.
3. *Whether anyone is born gay.* The answer here should be a resounding no. What is at stake is the denial of the right of SSA people to determine themselves differently. If one buys into the idea that sexual desire is immutable, all hope of change is lost and God is made to appear cruel.
4. *The possibility for someone with SSA to have an intergendered marriage.* For the third time, the answer here should be a resounding yes. This and the last question are the only two yes/no questions in the study guide. We should hold forth hope for the people to whom our culture now denies any hope of being different.
5. *Sodom and Gomorrah.* It is good to discuss the different parts of this image of dissolution given to us in Scripture. There is now a lot of misinformation in academic circles about the "real" sin of Sodom that is being disseminated through the culture, so it is good to go back to the texts about it and see that homosexuality is included as part of the destruction of God's image.
6. *How "gender asymmetries arouse."* This might be a delicate discussion to have, since we do not want to go too far into the bedroom, a place that should be shared only by a husband and wife. But it is helpful to recognize how certain differences are designed to spark healthy physical intimacy. Even housework distinction contributes to exciting sex.
7. *Eating chocolate with peanut butter.* This is just a fun question to lighten things up after the heavy topics of the evening.

Continuum of Closeness: When Gender Does and Doesn't Matter

1. *Old Testament and New Testament distinguishing gender outside of marriage.* The answer should be yes, and examples are given in the text. This question should help show, first, that gender asymmetry should be considered even outside of marriage, that is, in the church, because relationships range along a continuum. The closer the union, the more gender matters.

2. *Examples in your group's lives of genderly acts by spiritual or physical brothers and sisters.* Either in the church or in their biological family, hopefully folks can look back and see how gender came into play in an appropriate way. This discussion is important in our day to renew our appreciation for non-romantic intimacy, for fraternal benefits across the genders.

3. *Where gender does not matter.* If folks have grasped that relationships run along a "closeness continuum," and gender matters when you are close, they should be able to appreciate that the opposite is also true—sometimes gender doesn't matter or shouldn't matter. Examples include political candidates and workplace relations.

4. *Three ways for single people to experience intimacy.* Good to review: In their biological family. In their church. And in a special way with God. Singleness needs to be valued and praised for being, at the very least, an important phase at the beginning and end of all of our lives, but also, in the cases of unmarried adults, as a worthy and beneficial way of life. Talking about these pathways to intimacy can help.

5. *Valuing your singleness.* Can they? Expect a lot of different conflicting feelings among your single folks, especially those adults who wish they were married. It is a sore subject for them and they may be reluctant to talk about it. We need to try to bring it up in a way that they don't feel under a spotlight for not being married. But it is a good and revealing discussion to have.

The Immense Invitation

1. *Which role, husband or wife, is compared to Jesus Christ?* The answer is both: Ephesians 5:23, 2Corinthians 11:1-4, and 1Corinthians 11:3. So both men and women can identify with Christ, men with how Christ loves the church, and women with how Christ loves God the First.

2. *Ways Christ, as the Second member of the Trinity, acts genderly toward the First.* As folks think about it, they should be able to see how the Second submits to and promotes the First, how the Second came to make a home for Them on earth, and how the Second takes cues about Their mission from the First.

3. *The statement, "the more independent we become, women or men, the more intimacy eludes us."* Close living relationships seem harder to sustain in urban environments in our day, as interdependence becomes less valued by the culture. The situation may remind us of Jesus' words, "The love of many will grow cold." So it is understandable when people today are not able to achieve much intimacy in their lives.

4. *Ephesians 5 missions to which a husband and wife should more and more aspire.* To be a savior to his wife. To fear her husband. Discussing how can we do this, even though we are not God, should inspire us to love *like* God.

5. *What God ultimately wants for us.* To be caught up in the mutual love of the Trinity, to share what They experience among Themself.

Thanks for reading! May the Holy Spirit lead us all into the godliness and fellowship of the Great Three in One through the wonderful gift of gender.

Printed in the United States
By Bookmasters